EVAN

SOMEBODY 1
By Lia

FOREWORDS

"Liam has an incredible passion to help lost people find Jesus. In this book you'll learn much of his wisdom about turning that passion into a reality - something which he models both in his personal life and in the youth ministry he leads."

- Simon Benham, Senior Pastor
Kerith Community Church, Bracknell

"This book is a reflection of Liam's heart. He is a rare young man full of passion for souls. I believe you will be refreshed and impacted by the information and revelation that the book is loaded with. There is a dying world out there that needs Christians that are on fire to rescue them. This is just what you need to catch the fire to win the lost. This comes highly recommended."

- Dr. Kay Ijisesean, Author & President
KingsWord Ministries International

"Liam loves people and is passionate about telling 'somebodies' about a man called Jesus Christ who has the power to change lives. His love and passion are what drives him to pursue a lifestyle of evangelism and this book reflects his commitment, his thought process and his belief in the active sharing of his faith.

We all at times struggle to share our faith confidently but I believe this book will help you and give you the practical steps to share Jesus unashamed and boldly!"

- Dave Niblock, Youth Pastor
Life Church, Bradford

"Liam Parker is known for his desire to make the current world we live in align with the power and salvations revealed in the Gospels and in the book of Acts. He is passionate about seeing all, but particularly young people actively winning the lost and seeing the sick healed. This book sums together stories, teaching and practical advice on winning the lost, written with a heart to see all of us engaged in the Master's Business."

- Sola Osinoiki, Author & Elder
Kerith Community Church, Bracknell

ABOUT LIAM PARKER

Liam started as Youth Pastor for Kerith Community Church in 2009 and has seen Jesus do some amazing things amongst the young people. LIFE, the Kerith youth ministry, reaches hundreds of teenagers every week and to date, over 2000 young people living in Bracknell have heard Jesus preached at a LIFE event.

Liam also travels around the UK and internationally supporting youth ministries and preaching. He has a particular passion and focus on supporting youth ministries throughout Europe in order to see young people won for Christ.

Email: liam.parker@kerith.co.uk
Twitter: @ParkerLiam

THE IMPORTANCE OF EVANGELISM

A friend of mine named Amy once approached me saying 'Liam, I have figured out this Christianity thing!' Amy had been a Christian her whole life but had only recently started taking her relationship with God seriously and had clearly had a revelation about her faith! I replied to this bold statement by asking for an explanation and Amy began telling me that being a Christian is like a box of chocolates, the best box of chocolates in the whole world! She continued with 'our job as Christians is to pass on the chocolates to as many people as possible so they can experience the joy we have from eating them.' I didn't answer Amy straight away because this analogy didn't sit right with me, it just didn't seem serious enough or have a real sense of mission about it. I pondered over what she had said and replied with my own analogy. 'I think being a Christian is as serious as being a fireman. We are firemen standing before a burning building and our job is to run into the fire and rescue as many of the people who are trapped inside as we can!'

Amy demonstrated a very common approach to evangelism which I have called the 'chocolate' attitude. With this attitude towards evangelism and preaching the gospel you can get extremely comfortable. The 'chocolate' attitude is flawed because there are no consequences to not eating the chocolate, and in our society it is fine to not eat chocolate at all because chocolate is a luxury chosen by some rather than an essential needed by all. By taking this attitude with our evangelism and preaching we are reducing Jesus to something which is nice to have, but not a necessity. Finally we all know that if you eat too much chocolate you get sick, so by following this attitude we might think that we shouldn't talk about Jesus too much otherwise some people might get sick of it.

The 'fire' attitude, I believe, is a much healthier approach to evangelism. There was once a time when every single one of us was in the fire and someone helped pull us out, whether that was our parents, friend or pastor! We have all been there and now we are saved from it. It is now our turn to go in to help others know the freedom we have received. When you get pulled out of the burning building you are then trained up and given the right equipment to get back into the fire to help others. The fire attitude also demonstrates the urgency of our commission to preach the gospel to all creation (Mark 16:15). If someone is trapped in a burning building then firemen and civilians drop everything to help get people to safety; we too must demonstrate this urgency in our evangelism. Finally, with this attitude we must remember that like firemen, who go out in squads, we as Christians have our brothers and sisters with us in this rescue mission and we all need to work together to be as effective as possible to help others. We need to come to terms with the fact that people are in the fire and the only reason we haven't been called back to base is so we can rescue more people! This is an extremely challenging question but are we going to pull people out of the fire or are we going to stand by and offer them a box of chocolates?

BELIEVE IN WHAT YOU BELIEVE IN

'But in your hearts set apart Christ as Lord. Always be prepared to give an answer to everyone who asks you to give an answer for the hope that you have. But do this with gentleness and respect, keeping a clear conscience, so that those who speak maliciously against your good behaviour in Christ may be ashamed of their slander.'
1 Peter 3:15-16

As we look to evangelise to the people around us it is important that we understand what it is we are talking about. We are aware that it is about Jesus and salvation and has something to do with heaven and hell but the real question is why are we aware of these? Why do we believe they are truth? These are all true but it is important that we don't just tell people truth but that we lead them into truth. This is why some people who preach about the condemnation of hell on the high street don't see much fruit, it's not that what they are saying is untrue it's just that they are not helping the people understand why it is true! To help lead people into truth we must first understand how we were led into the truth and the best way to do this is to challenge ourselves and ask 'why do I believe what I believe?' 1 Peter 3:15 challenges us to be able to give a reason for the hope that we have in Jesus and to communicate this reason with gentleness and respect for the people who are willing to listen.

Each one of us should be able to share what we believe and why we believe it. Most people have some idea what Christians believe but don't know why we believe it! The why part helps lead them to an understanding of the truth and why it is so important.

Please note that while Peter challenges us to do this with gentleness this doesn't mean that we water down the message or make it more user-friendly. The truth is the truth no matter how you look at it. Peter is just reminding us that you can communicate the seriousness and danger of not knowing Jesus and still be respectful and gentle in your approach.

Whenever I teach a Religious Education lesson at a school my aim is to help the young people understand that there is some logic behind believing in Christ. My fear is that the younger generations see believing in Santa Claus and believing in God as the same thing. I inform them at the start of the lesson that I am not trying to force my beliefs upon anyone I just want the world to understand that there is logic and evidence in my life to have faith and believe in Jesus. I use the passage in 1 Peter as a guide at this point and have challenged myself to find out why I believe in God and have developed a small talk which clearly and logically demonstrates how, and why, I came to faith.

WHY I BELIEVE WHAT I BELIEVE

You can never know in advance how long you can keep a conversation going about Jesus, some people become extremely interested and are hungry to learn but others have a face that suggests they want to leave as quickly as possible. With this in mind I thought I would introduce you to the reason why I believe what I believe and the process I use when talking about Jesus so that I can communicate the gospel as logically, clearly and passionately as possible in as little time as possible. If needed I can run through this format in 2 minutes but I thought I would unpack it a little more with you today.

The process starts where my faith began, with the person of Jesus. The reason why I believe what I believe is because of Jesus. The theory of creationism did not make me believe and the answers to my questions on suffering did not make me fall to my knees. Only the love, grace and life of Jesus turned me from stone to flesh and opened my eyes to the image of the invisible God. My evangelism starts where my faith started, with Jesus.

JESUS AS A MAN

The logical place for me to start with an unbeliever is with the fact that Jesus was a man! I need to help people understand that we don't believe in fairy-tales or Santa Claus but that we put our faith in a man that really walked the planet, led a peaceful revolution and died on a cross. Historians would agree that Jesus actually existed and it is accepted as historical fact that he did die on the cross. There is a whole bunch of historical evidence stacked up in favour of Jesus, even more than other historical figures such as Julius Caesar. If someone still struggles to believe he was real then simply ask them what the date is and remind them that on the end of the year they should have A.D. A.D stands for Anno Domini, which is Latin for 'the year of our Lord'. So the calendar they set their life to is actually centred around a man named Jesus. Simply, he existed. However, just because he was a man doesn't mean he was a God, which brings us onto section number 2.

JESUS AS A GOD

This section is harder to prove with facts, figures and views of historians, however there are historical documents that have been written that talk about Jesus performing miracles. I find that this is not normally enough for people to accept Jesus as God though. For this section of our journey I would like to focus on the miraculous and supernatural element of Jesus' life to help prove his divinity. Why focus on miracles and the supernatural? because that's what Jesus used! You will struggle to find a page in the gospels where Jesus doesn't do something supernatural, it is a great demonstration of the power of God and it is hard to argue against a genuine miracle that happens right in front of your eyes. When evangelising I will always try and mention a miraculous answer to prayer I have seen and will always use the most legitimate, physical miracle I have seen.

For example; I saw a lady in our church healed of cataracts and she was able to see without her glasses immediately after we prayed, this was confirmed by the optician who was astounded at this miracle!

At this point people normally turn to me and tell me it is just a coincidence, which I always find funny because being healed of a serious eye condition and being able to see again after prayer is a really fortunate and cool coincidence. However, people normally need more proof and so I tell them as many miracle stories as they would like before they believe that it can't be coincidence. This normally helps people understand why I can believe in Jesus but it normally only takes them so far, it fails to help them see the importance of believing in Jesus for themselves! Jesus isn't a nice thing in my life that makes it feel more complete, Jesus is salvation for all and all need to believe. The next section helps us to achieve this.

I would like to throw out a challenge at this point. In the process of proving Jesus as God, it is extremely effective to have a story that you have personally experienced. I would encourage all Christians to regularly pray for the supernatural in their lives. Jesus and the disciples saw miracles on a regular basis and we should expect the same for our lives. Having a story of the miraculous that you were a part of and that you saw with your own eyes helps remove barriers of doubt in the unbeliever. If they refuse to believe your story then they have to come to the conclusion that you are either lying or that you are crazy. Hopefully as they have talked to you, they will realise that you are neither and therefore will be more open to believing that Jesus could be God!

WHAT DID JESUS DO?

Now that I have helped someone understand that Jesus is definitely a man and that he might even be more than a man I need to tell them of what he did so they can understand why it is so important for them to consider believing it for themselves. This is where the cross and Jesus' death comes into the conversation.

We all have our own ways of talking through the meaning of the cross but I like to start by making sure people are aware that sin and hell are serious problems! The truth is we have all sinned and no-one has reached the standard that God demands for us to join him in heaven, which is perfection. Therefore we are all in trouble and all of us are destined for hell. However, through the actions of Jesus on the cross, by paying our price for us and sacrificing himself, we now have a second chance to get into heaven! A chance that is based on our faith not our behaviour. Our faith in what Jesus did on the cross can justify us a place in heaven.

The fact that it can be so simple to secure a place in heaven normally astounds people. I have discovered that a lot of people thought it had something to do with behaviour and lifestyle, but when we show them that behaviour and lifestyle come after faith it opens up a new possibility for them. When people believe that going to heaven depends on their behaviour they rule it out as a possibility for themselves, however once they have a revelation that it is based on faith they start to believe that it might be something for them, that they might dare to accept Jesus and his offer of forgiveness.

WHY DID JESUS DO THIS?

My final part of why I believe what I believe is where I try to bring in the emotional side to our faith. Our faith is not all head knowledge but is really something in our hearts. I can't fully explain why I love Jesus so much but I just do, I feel it inside, I sense his presence and I am in awe of his life. It can be hard to explain logically to an unbeliever but I will try and end with the 'feelings' to show people how passionate I am about Jesus and that He really changes every aspect of your life.

Simply, the reason why Jesus came to earth, performed miracles and died on the cross was because he loved us! He couldn't leave us in our sin and he couldn't bear the separation from his children. He had to do something. At this point I hammer home how much God loves them and I will offer to pray and prophecy over them so that they might feel, sense or hear from God for themselves! I love this part and this is where the tears begin to flow and if God allows it you may see that moment in people's eyes when they realise Jesus is real and loves them.

I once remember watching one of our church elders praying for a new person after the church meeting. Before the prayer she had so many questions about God and because of this, struggled to believe. The elder then prayed that she might sense God's love for her. After the prayer her face had completely changed. Her eyes began to fill with tears as she had a 'heart' moment with God. She turned to the elder and told him that she now knows God is real, no major explanation she just knew. These heart moments are just as important as the head moments.

QUESTIONS

According to the Gospels Jesus was asked 183 questions to which he answered only 3 directly, the rest were answered by stories, parables or another question. Not only that but Jesus actually asked 283 questions. I figure that Jesus is actually trying to start a debate not end a debate!

When we evangelise as a Christian, especially in a school setting, it can feel that we are always on the defensive. We must answer all the questions that everyone throws at us and we must know the whole Bible otherwise we will let God down and we will lose the debate. I want to turn this on its head. One of the most effective forms of evangelism I have ever seen is asking people questions. Instead of trying to answer all their questions get them to answer some of yours. Who is Jesus? Why do historians believe in Him? Why do miracles happen? How come the majority of the earth believes in a deity yet you don't? I find that once you ask people to answer some of these questions they actually struggle.

Most people have rarely given as much thought to what they believe as a Christian, so when you start asking them what they believe and why they believe it, you can help them discover that they don't really know. This will actually help demonstrate to the people you are evangelising to that your faith is logical and you don't have to be crazy to believe it.

So my challenge to you is to stop worrying about having the right answer to end the debate and instead have the right questions to start one. To help you have the right question at the ready I suggest that you stick to asking people about Jesus. Jesus is very easy to prove historically and that will give you a good foundation to talk from. Also remember that there is power in the name of Jesus, simply saying His name can help change someone's heart and help change the atmosphere. Do your best to lead any debate or conversation to questions like: 'Who is Jesus?' 'What did he do?' 'Why did he do it?' and also 'What does Jesus mean to you?' Even if people start with a question like 'What about the Big Bang?' always try and lead it to Jesus, even if you have to say "I am sorry I don't really know about the Big Bang but I do know about Jesus can we talk about him?"

Finally remember that you don't have to defend the work of Jesus, Jesus does that. Remember the words of Charles Spurgeon -

'Suppose a number of persons were to take it into their heads that they had to defend a lion, a full-grown king of beasts! There he is in the cage, and here come all the soldiers of the army to fight for him. Well, I should suggest to them, if they would not object, and feel that it was humbling to them, that they should kindly stand back, and open the door, and let the lion out! I believe that would be the best way of defending him, for he would take care of himself; and the best "apology" for the gospel is to let the gospel out.'

10 STEP EVANGELISM

I once heard a teaching from an Evangelist named Adrian Holloway which was one of the most encouraging, simple and practical teachings I have ever heard on Evangelism and I would like to share it with you.

Adrian posed the tension that a lot of Christians don't evangelise because they feel the pressure of 'What happens if someone doesn't give their life to Christ?' 'Does that mean I have failed?' Because of this pressure some Christians just opt out altogether so that there can be no chance of failure.

Adrian then offered a solution to this problem. He showed us a diagram which has 10 steps on it. Each step represents a state of belief about the Christian faith. Starting with 1, which is someone who has no awareness of God up to step 10 which is a decision to surrender to Christ with 2-9 representing every stage in between. Have a look:

1. No awareness of God
2. Some awareness of God
3. Contact with Christians
4. Interest in Jesus Christ
5. Decide to investigate Christ
6. Grasp the truth about Christ
7. Understand the importance of this
8. Acceptance of Christian Truth
9. Acceptance of the implications
10. Decision to surrender to Christ

The idea behind this diagram is to encourage Christians to stop worrying about getting people to 10 and just help people take the next step up the ladder. Maybe by chatting to one of your school friends you help take them from 1 to 4, or perhaps the story you share with them sparks an interest in Jesus. Maybe when they are a 4 someone else might invite them to an event that talks about Jesus and because now they an interest, they attend the event! At that event maybe they jump to a 7 and understand the importance of Jesus. Then maybe while you are sitting in a maths class you talk to that same friend and you help them accept the truth of Jesus and they decide to follow him and reach number 10! You see everyone has their own journey they need to go on to accept Christ, it's not just about one moment or one chance encounter, for some it might take years of climbing up the ladder before they get to 10.

Take a moment to remember your own testimony, how many people helped you find Jesus? Very rarely does someone's testimony only have one person involved. If your journey involves more than one person don't be surprised when you're not the only person involved in someone else's. God is bigger than we think or remember. I hope you are encouraged by this teaching, just because you don't see your friend deciding to follow Christ after one discussion doesn't mean you have failed in evangelising because maybe you have just help take them a step closer to giving their life to Christ.

POWER OF PRAYER

In John 17:21 Jesus prays that his believers might reflect the relationship of that between Him and the Father and become one. One in their mind, spirit and purpose so that the world might believe that Jesus was sent by God.

We must strive to work together in unity to reach this world for Jesus but also persist in prayer to be in unity with God. Prayer helps shape us and sanctifies us to become more like Jesus, as well as helping us understand his will and the purpose he has for our lives. Just like a soldier is trained and given orders in the presence of his general, so Christians are shaped and directed in the presence of their saviour.

In Matthew 10:27 we are told to shout from the rooftops what Jesus whispers to us. This verse makes it apparent that the presence of prayer should be the foundation of evangelism for how can we shout from the rooftops unless we first allow Jesus to whisper to us in prayer. We must give time to God to give us the words to say so that when the right opportunity comes we know what to say and how to say it.

Finally we must remember that our prayers have power! James 5:16 tells us that the prayer of a righteous man is both powerful and effective. If we have been made righteous by the work of Jesus then we must expect our prayers to be powerful and effective. We have a weapon to use in our evangelism: we can speak against barriers that stop our friends from coming to Christ, we can pray for protection against the temptations of the enemy over our work colleagues and we can pray for people to respond to our invitations and expect the answer to be 'yes'. Let us pray without ceasing, as 1 Thessalonians 5:17 tells us, that we may notice the opportunities we have to witness, pray for the boldness to step out in those moments and pray that people might respond with a 'yes' and find righteousness for themselves through the work of Jesus.

COLD
EVANGELISM

WHAT IS COLD EVANGELISM?

In the rest of this booklet I want to introduce you to three forms of evangelism: Cold, Warm and Hot. Their name demonstrates how well you know the person you are trying to evangelise to. Let's begin with Cold.

Cold Evangelism is evangelism when you have never met or have only met a few times the person you are evangelising to. Cold Evangelism represents those times when you are asked to go out on the street and speak to people about your church or when you are at a party and someone asks you why you aren't getting drunk, or maybe even when you are sitting on the train and you start up a conversation with the person next to you about Jesus. This is Cold Evangelism.

I believe every Christian should have some experience with cold evangelism regardless of personality type or gifting. However we shouldn't be annoyed with ourselves if we are not out every single day praying for strangers. Cold Evangelism is arguably the hardest form of evangelism because it takes a lot of boldness to speak to strangers, let alone to speak to them about Jesus. It can also be particularly difficult in a culture where people can be very private and reserved and don't particularly like to talk about religion.

It is however important, and I believe that it helps challenge your faith as a Christian and push you outside your comfort zone, which is important because to reach the world for Christ we are going to have to step outside our comfort zones at some point. We normally leave this to extroverted, confident people but I believe every Christian, regardless of personality, should try Cold Evangelism for the main reason that you will be amazed at what God can do through you and how God leads you to certain people.

WHY DO WE NEED TO DO THIS?

I guess we could challenge ourselves with the question whether as a church we need to do/use Cold Evangelism as a way of reaching our communities? This would be my response:

I was walking along the road one day with a Christian friend of mine who decided he wanted to ask me some questions about my faith. He began to throw question after question at me: 'Do you believe in Jesus? Do you believe everything He said? Do you believe in heaven and hell? Do you really believe in heaven and hell?'

I replied, with a strong conviction, yes to all of his questions. My friend then pointed out a stranger walking across the pavement on the other side, he asked me 'if I believed in Jesus so much why don't I go and talk to him about Jesus and make sure he is a believer?' I had no response to this challenge, any excuse I came up with seemed rubbish in comparison to what death without Jesus looks like!

I had to question myself – 'Do I really believe in this stuff?!' After thinking about it I realised that in no way should I feel guilt about not approaching every single person I come in contact with and in no way should I feel that the burden of condemned souls is mine to carry! Jesus is the only one who can carry that kind of burden. However, I do feel like I should grow in my anguish towards people who don't know Jesus! I should feel a burning desire within me to communicate Jesus to as many people as I can in the most loving way I can. I know Christians who talk more about their football team or favourite TV show then they do about Jesus – I want to be different!

We need every form of evangelism we can get because so many people in our communities are living life without Jesus and will therefore die without Jesus. How can we sit on a train next to someone and not make sure they have a way to the Father! I realise that we can't do this every time we are on the train and I also realise that saving souls is our job, but ultimately God's responsibility but I want to be prepared, equipped and trained ready for that moment when God says 'speak to the taxi driver about me' or the person you are sitting next to on the plane says 'tell me about yourself?'. If I really believe in Jesus and believe in heaven and hell then why wouldn't I learn every form of evangelism so that I can be as effective as possible in spreading the forgiveness of Jesus Christ!

TIPS TO BE EFFECTIVE

One of my regular prayers is that God will continue to ignite a passion within me to see souls added to the Kingdom. However like any passion we must make sure that we have a way to focus it so that it can be most effective.

The Bible tells us that zeal without knowledge is not good. We need to have a huge zeal to see unbelievers take a step of faith into belief but we must also have knowledge about what it is we believe and how to effectively communicate that.

If we have knowledge without zeal then the truth is we will rarely step outside our comfort zone because only zeal and anguish will force us into situations that our knowledge alone wouldn't take us. I have a friend who was sitting at her exam desk in the middle of a big hall, with hundreds of other pupils, praying for her exam when God told her to drop to her knees and pray. Bravely she did so in the middle of the room. She received many reactions to that, none particularly nice. One of the examiners even told her she would be asked to leave if she did not sit back on her chair. Only zeal can push you onto your knees like that.

However zeal without knowledge can be damaging too. Zeal may push you to step out and approach people for Jesus, however if you don't have knowledge about what you believe or how to approach this person with respect then you can do more damage than good.

Let me illustrate it like this. Have you ever seen the film, cartoon or comic about the superhero team The Fantastic Four? If not then let me introduce you to one of the characters: Jonny Storm, the Human Torch. The Human Torch has a very cool, very powerful superpower where at any moment he can set his whole body on fire and use the energy from that fire to fly, shoot fireballs, melt pretty much anything and if he really wants, go supernova and basically destroy everything around him. Jonny's power is amazing and definitely very cool, however Jonny can turn the flame off which is just as important to Jonny as turning the flame on. If the flame was always on then he would burn down his house, no-one would be able to touch him and he would end up destroying everything he came in contact with! As you can imagine that would be a big problem. The flame-off is important because it allows people to approach him and get to know him without fear of being burnt.

In the same way, if we as evangelists are constantly talking about Jesus and don't engage with the world we can actually do more damage than good! If we are constantly in a state of depression or anguish over lost souls then we can actually isolate ourselves from the people we are trying to reach! We need to have a way of turning our flame on and off. We need to turn it off so that the world can feel safe to approach us to ask questions and just be able to get to know us. We need to turn it off so that we can keep ourselves engaged with the world and the people around us. However, this is not an excuse to not evangelise, we should always be ready to yell 'flame on!' and reveal our passion for Jesus. Just as Jonny would show off the powers and beauty of the Human Torch we can demonstrate the power and beauty of Jesus.

LESSONS LEARNT

When you are in a moment of Cold Evangelism, whether that be on an airplane or handing out a leaflet to your next Alpha course on the high street, it is important to always demonstrate love. We must remember that because we are approaching people for the first time it is imperative that they know we do this out of love, not judgement. If we stand on a box yelling at people that they are going to hell then we are actually just communicating judgement, how do we know people are going to hell? I can remember times when people have yelled at me on the street telling me that I am going to hell. I can even remember one time when I told them I was already a Christian and they said I should pray again to make sure! Do we really expect people to respond to judgement? Doesn't the book of Romans tell us that kindness leads to repentance?

I have to be honest and say that I have learnt this lesson the hard way. I have been out on the street and not demonstrated enough love and have ended up in arguments and hostile situations because I saw people as target to be achieved, rather than a person to be loved. One time I even had a person tell me 'You have no love in you' because of the debate that we found ourselves in. It hit me hard but it was true. In the moment when I told him that if he doesn't accept Jesus he will go to hell, I wasn't demonstrating love. When I went to God to repent for my behaviour I felt God point me towards 1 Corinthians 13 and had me read what love is. After reading it I felt the prompting to read it again but change the word love with evangelism.

Evangelism is patient, evangelism is kind, evangelism does not boast and it is not proud.

I realised that I need to base my whole evangelism strategy on love! I must be patient, be kind, not boast and not be proud!

Love can very easily be demonstrated while you are in a Cold Evangelism situation. It can be as simple as listening more than you talk, taking other people's views into consideration, smiling while handing out a leaflet and saying 'have a nice day'. But the best way I have found by far to demonstrate love for people in a Cold Evangelism situation is to offer to pray for the things they find challenging in their life. I once had a great opportunity to pray with a gangster who was on the run from his gang because he left them in hope that he might get to see his kids again. I prayed with him over lunch and after listening to his story we stopped and prayed that he might see his kids again after 2 years of running around the country without them. The very next day he found us again to tell us that he got a phone call out of the blue from a close family member and they told him he was going to see his kids that day! I even had the privilege of meeting his children and watch the smile fill his face! That guy proceeded to attend church and I even got to see him get baptised. There is power in Cold Evangelism to reach those that we would otherwise miss and to bring the Kingdom of God right onto the streets where we live, but let us make sure it is always done in love.

HOLINESS IS IMPORTANT

Hebrews 12:14 tells us that without holiness no one will see God! If we believe in the Bible then this can be a serious problem when it comes to evangelism! How can anyone see Jesus in us unless we set ourselves apart in holiness?

I saw this Bible verse in action the most when I was a teenager. When in school I made it very clear that I didn't drink alcohol at all, I wasn't going to have sex outside of marriage and that I didn't take drugs (please note I did this with a flame-off attitude and didn't go around shouting about it but when asked declared it with conviction). As you would expect this received many interesting comments and would even mean that sometimes I wouldn't get invited to the party. The reaction from people started with bewilderment, confusion, laughter and even worse, pity!

People were generally astounded that I would choose of my own free will, to live life like that. However as the years went on I demonstrated that I actually meant what I said by staying sober at parties and not having sex even though all my friends were starting too. As people saw me demonstrate this lifestyle their attitudes started to change. Rather than confusion I suddenly found people were interested in why I did this and why I would honour God in this way, people that would laugh would start to feel challenged to review their own lifestyle and people that showed me pity would come up to me at the end of parties and with a breath smelling of beer tell me how much they respected me for standing up for something.

I can remember countless conversations with people about Jesus which began with them asking about my holy lifestyle. Holiness is a great way to passively demonstrate the power of Christ and also quietens my selfish flesh to make way for the Holy Spirit to speak through me. I even remember one girl approaching me at a party shouting at me that she had always wanted to be virgin when she got married but somewhere along the line she had lost the hunger for purity in her life. I was able to chat with her and eventually pray with her to accept Jesus and help her regain her purity. I then remember taking a phone call from her boyfriend, which I assumed would consist of him yelling at me because I had convinced his girlfriend to stop having sex with him. However, to my amazement the boyfriend decided to follow her example and he later gave his own life to Jesus! Both still walk with Jesus now! Let me point out that the reason she approached me was because she knew I believed in the idea of purity and I believe in it so much that I lived it out. Would she have approached me if she knew I was sexually active? Would she have approached me if I was drunk that night?

By standing in holiness I allow Jesus easier access to my life and give him more space to work through me and when Jesus works through you people's lives are going to be transformed.

WARM
EVANGELISM

WHAT IS WARM EVANGELISM?

Second up, we have Warm Evangelism which is the middle ground between Cold and Hot, hence the title Warm. Warm Evangelism is used to describe those times when you invite a friend, colleague or family member to an event, group or party; for example a Christian concert or Christmas service. In Warm Evangelism there is normally an opportunity to discuss or talk about Jesus but no pressure attached to it, kind of like a free trial. You might find pressure when you are in a Cold Evangelism moment in the middle of the street asking a stranger whether they attend church, Warm Evangelism helps remove that pressure from the situation.

The Alpha Course is a great example of this. You invite a friend on a course with free food and a weekend away with moments where they can choose to openly discuss their views about faith, however, they are in no way pressured to do so. Warm Evangelism works well in a culture like England because culturally it can be inappropriate to approach people in the street and talk about religion. I have also noticed that the majority of people don't mind attending a free event, especially if there is free food!

In some ways modern church has become like this with a 'seeker sensitive' approach to services. These services allow people to attend and have a look at what all the fuss is about without having to make any form of commitment straight away. Some churches even allow people to serve and join teams as they start on the journey of discovering faith. I believe that every

Christian should be serving in some form of Warm Evangelism at their local church in some way. It is amazing to watch people's lives transformed as they attend Alpha or as they get hit with a God encounter at the seeker service.

You can also use Warm Evangelism in your personal life. I once took all my friends to Nando's and paid for them as long as they allowed me to say grace and I was allowed to talk about Jesus at the table. I also use it in schools with lunchtime clubs such as Jesus and Doughnuts. You can have a free doughnut as long as you come and listen to someone talking about Jesus for 10 minutes. Simple but effective.

WHY DO WE NEED TO DO THIS?

While visiting Isla Vista church in Santa Barbara, California, I witnessed a great example of Warm Evangelism which helps me illustrate why this is so important and can be so effective. I was invited along to a student prayer night where around fifty students gathered together to pray for their city and in particular the area they lived, a housing estate with only students living on it - a tough environment to witness about Jesus!

These fifty students had a very clever Warm Evangelism strategy to reach these students. Cold Evangelism may have been a bit tricky with the party atmosphere in the estate and Hot Evangelism (evangelism through an established relationship) may have taken too long as they would only be living in that area for 3 years at the most. However, a Warm Evangelism technique could prove very effective as the students offer something that other students wanted but were open that they offered it to show Jesus's love.

After the prayer meeting the students would go to the front of the house and start cooking a BBQ with hundreds of burgers, this was a free BBQ for anyone who wanted a burger! They would be out there all evening cooking burgers and any student walking past that fancied a burger could come and get one. The team would then spread themselves out and try and meet everyone and do their best to naturally bring up a conversation about Jesus! They cleverly named this technique 'Jesus Burgers', simple and effective. It definitely worked: when I was with them I met so many new people who had just come for the burger and every conversation I had I would end up talking about Jesus! Incredible.

They have seen some amazing moments and so many lives transformed that they have even written a book about 'Jesus Burgers'. The Warm Evangelism technique was a great way for this group of students to spread the word of Jesus to a tough environment in a way that was both loving and powerful!

TIPS TO BE EFFECTIVE

In Colossians 3:23-24 we are told to work with all our heart as though we are working for the Lord. I think this is a very good principle to add on to our Warm Evangelism technique. If we are going to invite people to an event where they will have the opportunity to talk about and maybe even believe in Jesus, for some of them this will be the first time they have had this opportunity, then we want to make sure that the event is at the highest standard it can be! We want the music to be played to a good standard and we want the place to be tidy and clean. I want the technical side to run smoothly and ultimately I want the team to work with their whole heart so that, as Paul says, 'that by all means we may save some'.

Before running or hosting some form of Warm Evangelism event ask yourself this challenging question: 'If Jesus came this evening would I be happy with the standard of our event?', and if you're not, then be bold enough to change it! We are not trying to impress Jesus or please him in this way but we should have such an awe and respect for the presence of God that we want to make the environment as good as we can. Just like Abel, I want to offer my first fruits, my best to Jesus. Why would I offer Jesus anything less than my best? It will take hard work and time to get there but I believe that it will be worth it.

If a young person walks into our youth event on a Friday night I want them to be so overwhelmed by it that nothing this world has to offer them will match us. I want our sound, lights, music and atmosphere to be better than the local night club so that they feel more inclined to come to our event. I want our church to be the place where you get the warmest welcome and feel most at home; I want our youth event to be the coolest place to be on a Friday night. I want everything we do to reflect the excellence and beauty of the person we do it for: Jesus.

LESSONS LEARNT

Keep it fresh – in matters of style swim with the current, in matters of principle stand like a rock.

While running the youth ministry at Kerith Community Church I have always tried hard to keep the LIFE youth event fresh and new, however in matters of principle we have always been firm. Every week at LIFE you will always hear a preach regardless of the event. If we are having a rave then halfway through the evening we will stop the music, make everyone sit down, we will preach for a good portion of time and then give time to pray with each other and allow young people to respond. This is a matter of principle for us and we believe this is what God has called us to do, according to Matthew 10. We will not be moved on this matter even if it means that people stop attending our youth event.

When it comes to matters of style we are happy to change and change again in order to keep our event fresh and keep the young people excited about attending. One way our youth ministry has changed quite a lot is actually not in what we do but where we do it. We discovered that some young people weren't always comfortable going to a church regardless of the fact that it was a youth event, so we decided to take the youth event to different venues in our community in order to reach new young people. We took the event to local schools so that young people would feel safe in a familiar environment and comfortable inviting friends along; we even hired a local nightclub in order to reach different people.

We can't be afraid of changing our event or taking risks on something or someone new. We will have moments of failure and we will try things that won't work but we must continue to adapt and change the style to stay relevant to the world that we are trying to reach.

HOT
EVANGELISM

WHAT IS HOT EVANGELISM?

Finally we approach Hot Evangelism, which is something I believe all Christians should be looking to live out every day of their life. Putting it simply Hot Evangelism represents friendship, it's a very relational form of evangelism. Hot Evangelism describes those times when you are building a relationship with someone that you hope will end up one day with you two praying the salvation prayer together.

Hot Evangelism is for the family members who aren't yet saved, the friends who already act like Christians but just don't believe and the colleagues you would love to see in church. It can even be for your husband or wife who still doesn't believe even though you have prayed for many years. It's that committed friendship that says 'I will be your friend no matter what but I would like to share my faith with you'. Evangelising in this fashion has some great strengths, there is a lot of space within the relationship for discussion and questioning. It is also really helpful because when you have a relationship like this you can accompany them to a Warm Evangelism event they might want to attend.

Although the number of people you can reach with this form of evangelism is limited it can be very effective and creates mature believers quicker than other forms of evangelism. The reason we see quicker discipleship development through this method is because when they are saved through a close friend or family member they have a spiritual mentor already there for them who can help them understand what the gospel is all about and answer any questions they may have.

WHY DO WE NEED TO DO THIS?

Hot Evangelism can be extremely effective and in some ways forces you out your comfort zone less than Warm Evangelism or Cold Evangelism. The huge benefit with it is that it helps create disciples of Jesus, not just people who responded to an appeal. If you visited our youth event regularly then you would start to notice that sometimes some of the young people respond to the salvation call multiple times before they really accept Jesus. Hot Evangelism helps avoid this because you have more one-on-one time to make sure the person understands what they are doing by accepting Jesus into their life. At our youth event now we often give everyone who responded one-on-one time with a leader who can go over everything with them. Even within Warm Evangelism events people may still need Hot Evangelism time.

If you have the honour of praying with your friend to accept Jesus you then have the amazing privilege of helping them understand how to live out their new found faith, and because they are connected with you they normally find it extremely easy to connect with your church and other Christian people because they have a friend to walk with them.

The effectiveness of Hot Evangelism can be described in another way. If everyone that attended my church, that's currently around 1,000 people, focused on building a relationship and talking about Jesus with one person every year then we could potentially double in a year. Not only would we be able to grow but we've already put the mentoring and discipleship structures in place to sustain it. We could put on a big show using the Warm Evangelism strategy and do loads of advertising to get two thousand to a church event, but to sustain that might mean that we have to continue to run that standard of event regularly. With Hot Evangelism anyone who attends the event or makes a commitment would already have a mentor in the faith and has an easy way to get connected into the church. The church could be both strong and big!

TIPS TO BE EFFECTIVE

Most importantly make sure you actually talk about Jesus at some point! I believe that we can settle into our friendships so much that we actually forget that there is this big elephant in the room and that at some point we need to talk about Jesus. This happens for many reasons: fear, familiarity and even comfort. I understand that we can't spend every moment evangelising to our friends, otherwise we might not have any friends! But we must not ignore the issue either. There is a different balance to each friendship about how much you can talk about Jesus, but we must never compromise the importance of the gospel out of fear of what a friend might say or think about us.

I would like to offer a very direct and dramatic challenge to you but one that is very true. All of your friends will either hug you or scream at you one day. They might hug you because you told them about Jesus and they are in heaven. You would have taken the risk, bitten the bullet and brought the Jesus subject up and they decided to listen and when they die they would have been greeted at the gates of heaven and welcomed in. They will now be in heaven and they will be so thankful that you took the risk! They will see how important it was and how real Jesus is. The other reaction you may receive will be them screaming at you 'Why didn't you tell me it was this important?!' they will be trapped in hell and we had the solution to this problem but we were never brave enough to risk our friendship to give them an opportunity. If your friend was going to drink poison wouldn't you try and stop them?

The danger is that we spend so much time building a relationship with them that we never get round to talking about Jesus or inviting them to church. We must go for it, even if it means an awkward conversation or even ruining the friendship. I once tried to evangelise to a family member after preaching one day but they told me they didn't want to talk about it and they walked off. Later another moment presented itself when we were in the car together stuck in a traffic jam and I realised that they couldn't walk away and that they would have to engage me on some level. I took the risk, knowing it would be awkward, and asked them to tell me what they believe about Jesus. To my shock they told me that they believe in a God and they had even prayed in the past! We can't be afraid to step into uncomfortable situations to win our friends for Jesus.

LESSONS LEARNT

In Matthew 10 Jesus instructs his disciples to wipe the dust off their feet if they are not welcomed in a town. I believe this principle can be very helpful when we are in Hot Evangelism situations. No matter how hard we try and how much we love, some people do not want to hear about Jesus, God or any form of faith. We have to be comfortable to say that that is ok and we are going to move on to tell someone else. Not that we stop being friends with them but that we focus our efforts on someone else.

I have had to fight the urge to chase people after they have left our youth ministry. A part of me wants to continue to try and meet up with them and try and talk about Jesus or text them every day with a Bible verse hoping one day they will respond and come back to church. This is certainly a noble thing but the problem is that there are so many people in the world to reach, is spending my time chasing someone who doesn't want to be chased an effective way of reaching the world? If people have said no to the gospel then that is their decision. We must respect that and move on to try and reach someone else. You have to decide, through prayer, when is the right time to move on.

We can't ensure that everyone says 'yes' to the gospel but we can ensure that everyone has a chance to give their answer. We must make sure that no one reaches hell without first of all being warned and being prayed for – Charles Spurgeon

Even Jesus didn't see a 100% success rate with regards to people believing in God. Jesus found himself in countless situations where people didn't believe in Him, one of his disciples even betrayed Him! Judas had spent three years with Jesus yet it wasn't enough for him to surrender his life to Him. If it happened to Jesus we must expect it will happen to us and we must learn to be comfortable with this fact.

I pray that these forms of evangelism will help encourage and equip you to see more people added to the family of Jesus Christ. The main lesson I have learnt about evangelism is to keep trying. Galatians 6:9 - Let us not become weary of doing good, for at the right and proper time we will reap a harvest if we do not give up.

ACTS 17:26 – PERHAPS ATTITUDE

Acts 17:26-27 'From one man he made every nation of men, that they should inhabit the whole earth; and he determined the times set for them and the exact places where they should live. God did this so that men would seek him and perhaps reach out for him and find him.'

I want to give you my last ounce of encouragement to get out there and evangelise by showing you these incredible verses. This passage tells us how God destined us to live where we live so that we and the people around us would reach out to God and find him. God planned for me to live in Reading in the U.K. and he planned that I would be born in 1988. He did this because this is the most effective time I could find him and help others find him. The people I went to school with, the people I work with and even my next-door neighbours were all placed there so that they could have the best opportunity to find Jesus!

Maybe you feel that you are not brave enough or that you don't know what to say or perhaps you feel that you are the least qualified person to evangelise. You may feel that because of mistakes you have made in your past that you have no right to talk about Jesus or maybe it just doesn't fit your personality type. If that is you then take encouragement from these verses. Your friends are your friends because God has destined it to be so! And he destined it because he knew that by being your friend they would have the chance to reach out and find him!

Notice how the verse says how men might perhaps reach out and find Him. God didn't destine everything so that people will find him; he did it that perhaps people might find Him. Perhaps is a phrase of opportunity; even though God has destined major parts of our lives he also leaves moments open to possibility. It is not a definite that just because your neighbour lives next door to you that they will become Christian, there is an element where we need to take responsibility in giving people a chance to find Him. We need to develop a perhaps attitude. I will pray for that person who is sick because perhaps they might be healed, I will say 'hi' to the person next to me on the train because perhaps they need someone to talk to, and I will offer to pray for my friend because perhaps he might just respond and offer his life to Jesus. We need to change our attitude when it comes to evangelism, yes it can be intimidating, yes it does take boldness, yes you might get rejected and yes some people will probably think you are weird. But perhaps some might find freedom in Christ, some might find a life-long relationship with Jesus which they pass on to their children, maybe you will see a miracle and maybe someone will thank you for stepping out of your comfort zone and introducing them to Jesus!

I remember once as I was walking to a church meeting with my friend and I asked God to show us someone to take with us. As we walked along we saw a man who looked to be in his mid-fifties. He was sitting on a bench looking upset and had a bag filled with alcohol sat between legs. My friend and I approached him and offered a listening ear, however he refused our help and seemed annoyed that we had spoken to him. We then said that we were going to a church meeting and asked if he wanted to come with us and to our amazement he agreed! We walked into the church meeting and he sat at the back of the room and began crying, the preacher then gave a call for salvation and to our absolute shock the man got up and marched down the front. My friend and I were totally blown away and confused by the whole situation so we approached him after the service to find out what had happened to him. He started by saying thank you to us for all we had done; my friend and I felt a bit strange because we hadn't done anything! He continued to say thank you to us and told us that we didn't understand. When we asked what it was we didn't understand he said that he had been planning to commit suicide on that night but because we stopped and brought him to church he now has a new life in Jesus. Amen! You never know what you will see or who you will help with a perhaps attitude.

31709063R00032

Made in the USA
Charleston, SC
26 July 2014